Belove

Remember This:

Before the first thought was Conceived

or the first form appeared

— the Infinite Self Is.

MOOJI

AN INVITATION TO FREEDOM

Immediate Awakening for Everyone

Mooji Media Publications

Revised first edition published in December 2017 by

Mooji Media Publications

an imprint of Mooji Media Ltd, UK
www.moojimedia.com | www.mooji.org

Ink drawings by Moojibaba
Edited by Gayatri, Jayani and Zenji | Cover design by Sido
Design support from Anna, Jyoti, Laura, Michel, Nitya and Rose
Photograph of Moojibaba by Reuben Steains
Printed and bound in Portugal by Gráfica Maiadouro

ISBN 978-1-908408-22-8   10   9   8   7   6   5   4   3   2   1

Salutations to

The Supreme Self

Jesus Christ

my Master Papaji

Ramana Maharshi

Nisargadatta Maharaj

Ramakrishna

Yogi Ramsuratkumar

all awakened beings

and seekers of Truth everywhere

Foreword

An Invitation to Freedom is a profoundly clear and direct pointing leading to Self-realisation. This unique guidance arose spontaneously in Mooji during his open Satsang season in Rishikesh, India, 2017. Simple in its language but extraordinary in its capacity to reveal the Real—that is, the unchanging and unborn awareness we are—the Invitation has ignited inside the hearts of thousands of seekers worldwide.

Mooji's pointing effortlessly cuts through the superficial veils that appear to hide the Self and swiftly introduces the mind to its source, the heart. It is recognised by today's seekers as a fresh and auspicious gift of grace from God—the Infinite Self.

Follow his guidance and experience the result today.

Introduction

*T*his little book is a celestial gem. It is an Invitation to real Self-discovery. It is your true companion. You could read through the entire book in a few minutes, but that would be to miss the magnificence it can awaken within you. So take time and sink into its embrace, and let it guide you Home.

An Invitation to Freedom truly offers immediate awakening to everyone who longs for Self-realisation. Many seekers expect to find awakening only after a long journey of spiritual study and practice. Here, we begin at the end, so that you cannot deny or doubt the obviousness and naturalness of absolute Being. And if there is any practice to be done, it will only be to fend off any habit that causes you to doubt your realisation of the Truth. Use this pocket book over and over again as your own mini emergency manual to freedom.

You may be surprised that the Invitation has the power to reveal the Truth so directly when it is generally regarded that awakening is rare, difficult and requires tremendous effort. Some even believe it is a myth. The world knows so few examples of liberated beings that the idea of Self-realisation seems inaccessible to ordinary people. Many feel it may even take us away from 'real life'.

But what we are searching for is already what we are—the ever perfect, impersonal awareness. As you follow the Invitation earnestly, you will recognise that what you are discovering is deeply familiar to you. The Truth that we are one indivisible Being, which the mind avoids and denies, is now being fully confirmed by your heart. True Being is beyond the rigidity of personal identity, or ego. It is timeless awareness—pure spirit.

Only the conditioned consciousness can evolve or be developed. The natural—the Supreme Self—can only be discovered. This quintessential understanding is the missing link, we could say, in the human expression of consciousness.

Nothing but the real discovery of the Self will satisfy humanity's deep longing and ultimate desire for lasting peace and happiness.

Each pointing within this book is essential and must be followed implicitly. Let the words enter your heart. Hear and feel them resonate within your being, the place of their origin. Don't move ahead until each sentence is felt, understood and confirmed internally.

Beware of the mind's tendencies to doubt, interpret or distort. Observe the ease and simplicity with which the guidance flows within you, like water being poured into water.

As the Invitation blossoms inside, keep confirming it whenever you can, to your heart's joy. Any mist will quickly clear as the true Self, the Is-ness*, keeps revealing itself as the ever present, all-encompassing reality.

* **Is-ness:** Mooji uses this term to point to the ungraspable, all-encompassing reality. Since it is indefinable, 'Is-ness' is to be understood more like a formless noun, pointing to the ultimate Self that we are. It is also referred to and known by many other names such as pure Awareness, God, Truth, the Tao, Brahman, paramatman, Supreme Spirit, the source, pure consciousness, the Supreme Being, the Absolute Self.

"Don't give it any shape. Is-ness, or pure awareness, is beyond names and forms. It is unfathomable to the mind. It is the essence, unimaginably Real—timeless, unborn, imperishable." ~ Mooji

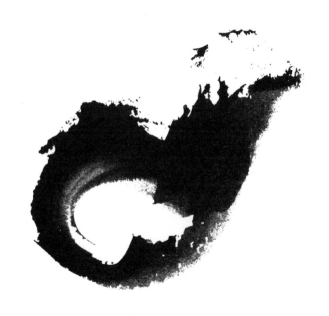

The Invitation

*T*oday we are here to discover our very own Being, that which is Real and in accordance with the insights and direct experience of the greatest sages and seers of all time. Through the grace of the Invitation, we too will directly experience that the one Self alone exists and that we are one with It.

If you are longing for Self-discovery and the urge to be free is alive and compelling, this Invitation is for you. Grace has put this yearning inside your heart, and so it is possible to come to this direct recognition without delay. It works, it works, it works—yesterday, today, tomorrow and always.

Let's begin.

You say, '*I want to discover the Truth as it really is. Please help me. I want to know and be who or what I truly am, not my ego and conditioning.*

I want to meet, know and be in harmony with God, the Truth. I want to be real and be finished with what is false. I don't want to waste any more time. My life, lived in the notion of a person, is not really working. It kind of works, but it is missing the joy, wisdom and love that I see in you and your students. I wish to wake up today to the unchanging perfection that you point to and that I witness in you, who expresses it so naturally. I want to be in that state permanently. Can you help me?'

From the room of my being I invite you, 'Come in, but before you enter please leave your shoes outside.

One more thing: also leave your mind outside, because there is no room in here for thoughts.'

'But how to leave my mind outside?' you ask.

Leaving the mind outside simply means leaving the mind aside. Leave aside all that you believe you are and all that you think you know about yourself and about life.

I ask you to do this just for the short duration of this guidance.

Leave all thoughts about the past and any memories which tie the mind to the past. Past has passed—that's why it's called past.

Don't touch any concerns about the future also, for no one has ever experienced the future they imagine. The actuality of the moment is always different from the projections of the mind.

Leave aside even the present moment.

What I mean is that we don't need to refer to any of these things now. They are not important for finding freedom and mostly they just get in the way.

For now, let's brush all these things aside. Stand apart from events and time. Be entirely empty and free.

Can you accept this?

Also, don't cling to any dream or desire, for instance what kind of world you'd like to live in or the kind of person you'd like to be.

All our desires and attachments are based upon imagination and conditioning, or they come from what we have read and heard. Is there any truth in them? Maybe, but right now, I'm asking you to step out of the mould and leave everything behind.

Please trust this.

Continuing, leave your personal sense of self outside also—that is, who you believe yourself to be. Now, some resistance or fear is likely to come up from time to time; this is to be expected. So don't panic. Stay with my guidance and don't be distracted. It is important to be completely empty. You will soon see why.

When we are finished you may re-identify with the person and its world if you wish. I promise that they will be waiting for you right where you left them, but only if you want them back. If you don't want them, you will find that they don't actually exist.

Shall we move on?

You don't need to create, imagine or visualise anything.
So don't worry, you cannot fail. You are not required to do
anything at all. In fact, you are going to find that leaving aside
everything is easy and natural.

For now, leave aside even the desire for enlightenment itself.
Trust this. Leave all these ideas that we have wrapped around
ourselves. Don't get entangled with the mind.

Stay as you are.

Isn't it a relief?

Now as you enter, you are empty. Welcome.

Remain empty, like zero, beyond even the concept of empty or zero. Now you are without history or content. Feel this.

Don't go backward or forward and don't pick up any new concepts or ideas. The old regime of personal identity and its ways we have left behind.

You are now inside the heart as the heart itself.

Simply rest in and as what remains by itself. This is your natural state. Remain like this.

See there is no next thing to do or undo. There is no time, no past, no future, no self-assessments, no comparisons, no expectations. You are beyond form, indefinable, but fully here. Don't rush and don't involve the mind.

Allow some space around this discovering.

In this unbound space, recognise that you are not 'holding yourself together' or managing your existence. Each thought, feeling and sensation is like a cloud passing. You are like the sky: vast and unchanging.

Notice the limitless space of formless awareness, just the sense of Is-ness—natural, silent and empty. It is nothing in particular. It is just What Is. 'What was' and 'what could be' have floated by. Nothing sticks.

Notice that you are not waiting. Notice also that you are clear-minded and not in some imaginary state. There is only the space of formless awareness. You are naturally self-aware. Perceiving happens effortlessly, yet you are neither creating nor collecting. Immaculate.

The mind might say, *'This is boring! There's nothing here! What's the point? We're not getting anywhere. This is all just talk. It's not helping me.'*

It is vital to not get pulled into the mind's web. Don't trust it, don't believe it, don't engage with it. And don't be discouraged or distracted. Mind is simply trying to trick you into becoming personal again so that you remain unaware of your true state and power as unborn awareness. Mind gains life for itself by deceiving you.

Notice that mind can only attack the idea you have of yourself and not your true Self, which is beyond its reach. You are the formless intelligence in which all this appears, yet your Self remains unblemishable.

Feel what it is just to be. You are effortless existence. 'To be' is not an instruction to be carried out. You are not 'going to be' or 'become'. There is nothing to construct or change. There is nothing to add. You are already complete.

Isn't it now becoming obvious? Be one with this knowing.

You are now in the natural, egoless space—unbound. Take a little time to confirm and digest your experiencing.

I had to invite you here so that I can ask you a few simple but important questions. Each and every question facilitates the direct experience of your true Being. They don't compel you to think or learn but to discover, and reveal the ultimate Truth. Notice also that the contemplation of each question takes place inside the unchanging, limitless space of Is-ness.

Don't move from one question to another until you grasp what is being asked. Your responses should flow from your direct insight and experience—straight from the heart.

Follow earnestly. Read slowly. Please don't hurry.

This space that is effortlessly here,

which I refer to as Is-ness,

though indescribable, it is fully alive, isn't it?

—like some kind of ungraspable intelligent vastness.

Are you aware of this?

Is the Is-ness an object? Is it a feeling?

Could it be described as active or passive?

Is it male or female?

Does it have limitations or any boundary
beyond which it is not?

Does it have an image or form?
For instance, can it be photographed
or captured in some way?

Does it have desires, attachments or fears?

~<

Can the Is-ness belong to or be owned by any person,
religion, philosophy or doctrine?

Can it become emotional?

Can Is-ness be insecure, angry or jealous?

Does Is-ness require or depend upon belief?

Can it become sick?

Or can it suffer or cause suffering?

20

Can it be for or against anything or anyone?

Does the Is-ness have needs, or can it lack anything?

Can Is-ness be distracted?
Can it have problems?

Can Is-ness be influenced or manipulated
in some way?

Can it be bound or liberated?

You are in the perfect place to know this:
Was Is-ness born? Can it die?
Reflect.

You are discovering the Is-ness now,
but where has it been all this time?
Can it leave or fade? Where would it go?
Is there a place where Is-ness is not?

Can the mind function outside of Is-ness?

Is Is-ness personal?
If it is not a person or any other object of perception,
how is it being recognised?

Can the recognition of Is-ness happen outside of or apart from the Is-ness itself?

Finally, is there any distance between what you are and Is-ness?

*I*f there is no distance or separation between you and Is-ness, then all your responses must be about You, and they must be arising directly from the Is-ness—your real Self. Is this too big a discovery for you to bear? And who would you be to bear it?

The recognition of Is-ness must obviously be a non-phenomenal recognition. This means it is a non-visual or invisible recognition, for how else can that which is formless be recognised?

Is-ness cannot be recognised by anything other than Is-ness itself. Therefore, Is-ness and your Self are one.

Be confirmed in this

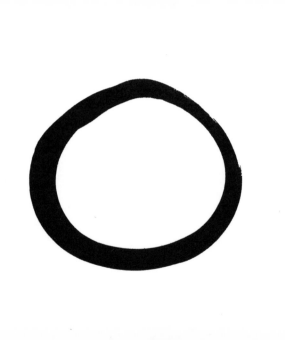

*Y*ou have been introduced to your own pure Being. Have you ever felt more peaceful, content and complete than you do now? Recognise that you are not a visitor here.

This is your true place. This is your true Self.

Become accustomed to remaining one with the Is-ness as Is-ness itself. Bring your attention to it. Stay with it. Acknowledge it. Love it. Enjoy it. Be it. Finally, even this effort falls away and the self-evident Truth shines as unborn awareness—the one true Self.

Enjoy your Freedom. Enjoy your Self.

Timeless love,

Moojibaba

And then…
(Important pointers against the backlash of the ego-mind)

*E*ven after such a profound seeing, many, if not most, seekers will experience a backlash from the ego-mind. Due to the force of habits, the reflex to re-identify as a personal self will keep arising from time to time.

But if you remain impersonal—that is, you don't identify with the ego—it will be seen that these habits are mere superficial movements inside the unmoving Is-ness you are. No matter what, remain one with the Is-ness which is your source Being.

The power of Truth is with you.

If something seems to go out, notice that it is only the habit of attention moving towards personal identity. But even if such a movement occurs, it is quickly recognised within the expanse of the Is-ness, and thus neutralised. The one true Self remains as it is—unchanging and untouched, yet fully alive, as the source of the mind itself.

Through the Invitation, the ego's delusive power is being cut at the very root—and it will fight to protect its psychological life. Whenever it finds the opportunity, it will re-present the most vulnerable states of the person you imagined yourself to be.

Avoid this trap of the ego-mind by recognising that the person, your old self-image, is an observable phenomenon witnessed in and by your true Self, the unborn awareness.

Anticipate ego's cunningness and you will find yourself ahead of its game. Even though the heat of a mind attack may be experienced with great intensity or discomfort, don't panic. It is neither an indication that freedom isn't for you nor that you are failing. In fact, it is quite the opposite. It means you are on to something and mind feels threatened.

Be clear about this: such attacks can only happen to the person and not to the real Self. Actually, they serve in exposing where egoic identity and its tendencies are still hidden or being preserved inside yourself. Knowing this, don't despair. Rather, be encouraged and feel the joy of merging with the Self.

You are recognising that there is only the one indivisible Self. If the sense of an attack is experienced, who exactly is being attacked and who is the attacker? Can either be found?

Contemplate this and you will recognise that all conflicts are between forms, and all forms appear inside the formless. How paradoxical that our most firm ground is in formlessness. You must keep confirming your true position as the formless witness until there is no space left for an imaginary self to hide or persist.

Finally, all suffering comes to an end when we awaken from the long and tiresome dream of separation into unborn Awareness—the Supreme Self.

An Invitation to Freedom

is also available as an audiobook from

www.mooji.org/shop

About Mooji

Mooji's presence and love have the power to lift one effortlessly into the experience of the higher Self even from a single encounter. He lovingly guides the many seekers who come to him from all parts of the world in search of the direct experience of Truth. In these spontaneous interactions, the directness, wisdom and humour of his pointings easily dispel delusion and thus quicken the recognition of the infinite Self we all are. Mooji presently lives in Europe and occasionally travels around the world sharing Satsang.

Further details about Mooji's work
and schedule are available at:
www.mooji.org

Satsang recordings in audio and video
formats can be found on:
www.mooji.tv
www.mooji.org/shop

Mooji is also on YouTube:
www.youtube.com/moojiji

and Facebook:
www.facebook.com/moojiji

For Mooji's other books

Vaster Than Sky, Greater Than Space
The Mala of God
White Fire
Before I Am (2nd Edition)
Writing on Water
Breath of the Absolute

you are welcome to visit:
www.mooji.org/shop

For additional information and enquiries
about books please contact:

Mooji Media Publications
office@moojimedia.com